DEPARTMENT OF EDUC

TEACHING

POETRY

IN THE

SECONDARY

SCHOOL

An HMI view

LONDON: HER MAJESTY'S STATIONERY OFFICE

ISBN 0 11 270596 0

Contents

In practice you hear it coming from somebody else, you hear something in another writer's sounds that flows in through your ear and enters the echo chamber of your head and delights your whole nervous system in such a way that your reaction will be 'Ah, I wish I had said that in that particular way'. This other writer, in fact, has spoken something essential to you, something you recognise instinctively as a true sounding of aspects of yourself and your experience. And your first steps as a writer will be to imitate, consciously or unconsciously, those sounds that flowed in, that influence.

SEAMUS HEANEY[1]

There is only one trait that is common to all poets, without exception, a passionate love for their native tongue. This means that the phrase 'poets are born not made' must be false, for babies are born speechless.

W H AUDEN

The teacher must love poetry but must not be a Poetry Lover, must never try to turn the thing into a sacred cow.

VERNON SCANNELL

I think with a poem, it's very important that you can have it all packed in, full of all the things you wanted to say... I think that's what attracts a reader, what it sounds like, the way it's written, the sort of flow of words.

EMMA, *aged 10, in a Nottinghamshire primary school*[2]

1

Introduction

POETRY MATTERS because it is a central example of the use human beings make of words to explore and understand. Like other forms of writing we value, it lends shape and meaning to our experiences and helps us to move with confidence in the world we know and then to step beyond it, to respond to the generation of meaning through significant, memorable and deliberated kinds of language. It is an activity to which we are drawn because in its range and rigour we feel both the presence and the pressure of human experience. Poetry embodies delight in expression, stretched between thought, feeling and form. As we become aware of the 'true soundings' of poetry so we become aware of what we ourselves might do with language.

Poetry includes a concept of human creativity and imagination and a notion of energy and value. For poetry is, in essence, engaged with the living situations of men and women, with the shape and motive of human conduct and with the language that creates the sense of the rich variousness of that living. Poets work at the frontier of language. They are engaged with the struggle for clarity and meaning and those who wrestle with and refine language in order to be lucid and articulate are, in a crucial sense, the guardians of the accumulated richness of our written and spoken inheritance.

There has never been any serious challenge, since English came to be considered a suitable subject for the classroom, to the view that literature, including poetry, should be at the centre of its preoccupations. For something over a hundred years large and passionate claims have been

1

made for it. Literature has been seen by some as most valuable when, standing aloof from the strife of nations, class or party, it promoted social and cultural harmony by its supposed distance from the day-to-day world. It was been seen by others as an agent of social enlightenment, liberalising, through its polite pleasures, minds otherwise narrowed by the pressures of commercial and professional life. The appreciation of literature has been believed to have a softening effect, especially on women, whose training for wifely duties required them to be able to dispense sizeable portions of sympathy and understanding! As a witness before a Royal Commission in 1877 put it: 'Literature is a suitable subject for women and the second and third rate men who become school masters.' The 'civilising charms' of literature have been believed to promote quiet peaceful study and self-improvement, disposing the reader to good order and discipline.[3] Literature has been further and variously seen as a counterweight to technical learning, a substitute for classics and religion in engendering social reconciliation, an organic 'national' tradition, a means of survival in a philistine mass society and a way of restoring meaning in a fragmented world. The study or criticism of literature has itself been given a wide role, from the necessary ground clearing which must precede full artistic flowering to an activity which could transform the deadening effects of an industrialised society.

It is also fair to say that literature has become institutionalised in education and that around the reading of books there has grown a whole structure of secondary activities – glossaries, paraphrases, analyses of plot, character studies, biographies, background studies – which have severed the connections between literature and the language and experience of reading, so that the image of literature in many pupils' minds is of a form of knowledge to be examined, like many others in the curriculum, rather than of a man or woman sitting down with pen and paper and making something in a common human idiom. It is this which provides the context for Adrian Mitchell's refusal to let any of his work be used for the purposes of any examinations whatsoever and Shaw's 'eternal curse' on anyone who should make his plays hated as Shakespeare is hated.

The sharp severance that often exists in schools between the study of language and the study of literature suggests that literature is a special and select activity carried out by a few established writers which has few connections with the uses made of language by pupils or with the language of home, community and ordinary living. When reading is set apart from writing, or everyday speech from literature, pupils do not see literature as part of the universal uses of language, more subtle and deliberate perhaps than everyday expression but essentially hand in hand with it. The roots of what we call literature are in everyday stories, dramas, rhythms, songs, rhetoric and the flow of language in relationships. In the shaping and making of their insights to be communicated, it is important that pupils perceive that whenever they write they are sharing the medium with those whom they may regard as writers.

Poetry needs to be at the heart of work in English because of the quality of language at work on experience that it offers to us. If language becomes separated from moral and emotional life – becomes merely a trail of clichés which neither communicate with nor quicken the mind of the reader – then we run the risk of depriving children of the kind of vital resource of language which poetry provides.

As teachers we are concerned not so much with the numbers of words potentially available but with the degree to which the resources of language are put to current use by our pupils. Among other things, literature is, as Ezra Pound argued, a way of keeping words living and accurate. It is the place of poetry in English teaching to help us to restore to pupils a sense of exuberance and vitality in the acquisition of language and in the power and savour of words.

2

Making readers
– the pool of language

Let (the pupil) read – let him wander with it and
reflect upon it and bring home to it and prophesy
upon it and dream upon it.
Keats *Letters*

TED HUGHES in his important and influential book *Poetry in the making*[4] described two aspects of poetry that seem to him to be central. His first claim is that poetry is possessed of 'a certain wisdom, something special, something that we are very curious to learn'; his second is that the latent talent for self-expression in any child is immeasurable. These recognitions are at the heart of reading and writing poetry in schools and the activities in the classroom need to reflect a desire to promote both, in a collaborative endeavour between teacher and pupils.

However, the current state of the teaching of poetry in many secondary schools does not show much faith either in the wisdom of poetry or in the powers of self-expression of the pupils. Inspection of and visits to secondary schools indicate that there is in many of them very little poetry included regularly in the work in English. The findings of specialist one day visits and a number of full inspection reports show that poetry was at the centre of work in English for rather less than five per cent of the English lessons observed. The evidence is that, in national terms, poetry is frequently neglected and poorly provided for; its treatment is inadequate and superficial. Many pupils spend much more time completing language exercises of little value than they do reading, writing or talking about poetry. They are very much more likely to be given a course book for work in English than they are to be given an anthology of poetry or the opportunity to read widely in the work of particular authors.

Some English teachers express great unease about teaching poetry and it appears that there are few genuine enthusiasts who read poetry extensively themselves and communicate that enthusiasm to pupils. The reasons why some teachers seem afraid of poetry are not easily discerned but it is clear that choosing and presenting poetry is not as easy as presenting fiction and that teachers are often aware of a background of hostility to poetry among their pupils. There is the danger of a self-defeating process here and it is notable how few English departments, through their guidelines, meetings or discussion papers, have faced the problem directly. Most English department documents have little to say about the teaching of poetry. It is recognised in many as being a good thing – 'Poetry should be encouraged wherever possible' – but the resources and methods for that encouragement are not detailed. Some schools see the teaching of poetry as an apparently straightforward task of escorting pupils through a formidable barrier of technical terms – 'In this year metaphor, simile, onomatopoeia, assonance, alliteration, synecdoche and oxymoron will be taught' – and in one school there they were, defined, copied out, learnt for tests, with not a single reference to a complete poem. Many schools have large stocks of old anthologies which are never used, and it is not uncommon for modern anthologies, containing material that would extend and deepen pupils' experiences of poetry, to lie idle in English department stockrooms.

Teachers' attitudes to poetry are crucial: in the importance they attach to it; the enthusiasm with which they read it aloud; the extent to which they read it widely themselves; and the way in which they demonstrate a concerned responsibility for it – in short how they give it rank and status. The message children receive about poetry from its placing in most course books is clear enough: it comes a poor third behind the 'For written answers' section and 'Find out more about' demands. Teachers should not themselves reinforce that message by relegating poetry to the end of the day or the week or the term, when resistance is low and all the 'essential business' of English has been completed.

It is dispiriting to note that in general terms the features of the teaching of literature noted in The Bullock Report[5] in 1975 have not changed to any marked degree as far as the teaching of poetry is concerned – 'The explanations and the summaries have expanded to take-over point; the literature has receded'. The treatment of poetry as 'little more than comprehension passages', the proliferation of 'model answers, stereotyped commentaries ... with no hint of felt response' have persisted in creating unsympathetic attitudes to literature in the minds of many secondary school pupils. There is evidence for this in the statistics of APU's first Secondary Language Survey[6], where 47 per cent of pupils indicated that they read no poetry out of school; 73 per cent indicated that they did not read poetry to any great extent; and 36 per cent were completely hostile to it. Alternatively the matter comes sharply into focus in the comments of one fourth year O-level pupil: 'If I was given the choice of never to do poetry again, I would not do it. In my whole life, reading poetry – never have I enjoyed it. I would arrange separate classes for children who wanted to do it.' The pressure of the syntax gives the sense of desperation and it is a chilling irony that, however well intentioned teachers of English have been, they have often failed to disarm indifference, resentment and hostility. For many pupils, poetry has not been a series of experiences where the young reader could find a mirror of some of his own feelings and preoccupations in a common human idiom. If this is to happen it must be recognised that it will not happen by chance (although room should be left for the chance encounter) and that approaches to poetry in the classroom must be at least as clearly structured and provided for as other aspects of English, if they are to impart a sense of pleasure and direction.

The ways in which meaning is established for the reader of poetry in the classroom depend upon the associations and contents of the language of the poem reaching into the reader's mind. So although the initial engagement of the reader with the poem is a private affair proceeding at an area below articulation, it issues finally in language that reflects an active process which has taken place in the reader's mind – a mental travelling, which we can call response, judgement or understanding. Above all, pupils need time to make their own responses, to assimilate and ponder before being plunged into talking and writing about what the poem means. Thereafter this opening up of a poem and the exploration of its meaning depend upon the sensitive direction of a teacher concerned about both the language of the poem and the responses of the pupils as they approach the poem, in George Herbert's phrase, as 'a box where sweets compacted lie' whose unpacking is a process full of pleasure and satisfaction.

One or two examples may serve to illustrate this process. In the first,

6

a group of third year pupils were given copies of Kit Wright's *January Birth*. The teacher read it aloud twice, with a short pause between readings.

JANUARY BIRTH [7]

for Caroline Maclean

Brightest splinter, scarlet berry,
  On the shivered world you lay,
Sliver from the tree of winter
  When the hawthorn held no may,
When the city plane was childless
  And the dark was in the day.

From her labour then your mother
  Freely wept to see you wake,
Take this crying star for neighbour:
  Wept with joy for your fierce sake,
Heart of light in snowing darkness,
  Storm of love and glistening flake.

O tender head, bare tree that branches
  Veins in perilous array,
May the violent day defend you.
  Want for nothing, little clay.
O cup of air, O moth-light wingbeat,
  Darling, bear the world away.

Working in small discussion groups the pupils were instructed to consider and 'unpack' the poem's meaning and to choose one person from the group to report back to the class at the end of the lesson. The language in the groups was initially tentative but one group moved carefully from what they knew to what confused them. 'Scarlet berry', 'tree of winter', 'dark was in the day' were agreed upon as being clear but it was interesting to see how ideas were connected – holly and the winter tree contrasting with spring and the may blossom and with the darkness of the day. This led to a sudden excited sense of why 'Brightest splinter' opened the poem and how the child was a 'sliver' and what a 'sliver' meant in the context of the poem. The discussion shifted to the third verse because of the word 'tree'. One girl immediately saw the 'branches' of veins by pointing them out on her forearm, followed by absorbed comparisons. A boy who had been very quiet said that he was frightened of young babies because they looked as though they could be so easily hurt – 'perilous, like it says'. Some anecdote followed. One girl said she thought her older sister was frightened of her baby when it was very young because she had looked so tense and anxious. Someone suggested that she might be frightened that something would happen to it but would not be frightened of it. 'What about joy?' someone asked. 'Is it a joyful thing, a new baby?' and attention returned to the poem and the second verse. The group agreed readily on why the mother cried – the sense of relief, the first cry of the child, the desire to hold the child tightly – 'the storm of love'. They could not decide whether the star was crying in sympathy for the mother's joy or whether it simply looked like a tear and they thought it might be a mixture of both. 'I like the last line' said a boy, at random, 'after all the world is yours when you're born, you could become almost anything.' At this point the teacher asked for the group contributions and a pattern of reading and understanding emerged. There was common agreement that the child was precious and its life contrasted with the darkness of winter; that it was like the holly because it had colour and vitality, that it was vulnerable and helpless, a joy to its mother, delicate but full of a sense of the future. As one group said, 'It is the future, like the New Year is presented in cartoons as a baby.' Two groups particularly liked the rhythm of the poem. The teacher then set some writing arising from ideas or situations suggested by the poem, although writing need not always be the ineluctable outcome of such reading and talk. One girl began a description of her mother; a boy started a script which took place in a park as two fathers met, with new-born babies in prams, and talked about their hopes for their babies' futures. One boy wrote about a winter landscape, and remembered seeing a Breughel nativity illustrated in a poetry book of which this poem reminded him. Two pupils began poems, one entitled *Winter Trees*, the other *Nursery Song*. (Neither pupil, incidentally, was aware of Sylvia Plath or William Blake.)

What emerged from this is not necessarily a model of successful practice, but it illustrates the effective establishment of meaning and the generation of language in pupils. That members of the class took on new ideas from the experience of reading the poem was important but the sharing of ideas and insights confirmed that reading poetry is not a passive activity and that children need to be encouraged to bring a careful and thoughtful attentiveness to the way they read.

Another example of the carefully constructed approach to a particular poem, designed to encourage pupils to read fully and well, took place in a fifth year English literature class where pupils were studying a selection of Hardy's verse. The pupils were asked to collect anecdotes about themselves when young, from parents, grandparents or any other relatives; a memory which was established in the older person's mind as something they would never forget, but which the pupils themselves did not remember. These were recorded on tape by the pupils, to produce about half an hour's programme of anecdote and reminiscence, recorded by a person involved in the incident but who had been unaware of it at the time. The tape itself was full of interest and the teacher followed it by asking pupils to identify common themes or patterns in the reminiscences. A number of pupils identified a concern with parties, Christmas, family occasions, holidays and starting school; and as they talked it became clear that they detected a certain melancholy beneath what was often funny, disarming and intimate. There was a tension between the re-telling of the incident and an awareness that it had passed and, in a poignant way, was beyond reach: a lived experience with differing degrees of significance for the different participants, with the child, the centre of the incident, unaware at the time of its occurrence of the part he was playing. It was only at this point that a poem from the Hardy selection was introduced and rooted in a number of ideas and observations that had emerged from the discussion – namely that 16 year old pupils themselves had a past which was built into someone else's emotional response to that past, and that memory was a source of subtle emotional ambivalence. In the Hardy poem *The Self Un-seeing* there was, for those pupils, a sense of recognition both of self and of situation. The Hardy poem, instead of being perceived as something selected for a distant examination and written by a dead poet, became a living voice, sharing and articulating feeling. Pupils recognised in short the wisdom which Ted Hughes claims for poetry. In the writing about the poem which followed there was a warmth which reflected and grew out of this engaged reading, in marked contrast to the dead prose paraphrases that so often diminish the language and ideas of poetry. Though not required to do so, one girl wrote a poem, stimulated by the vision of her own past.

A photograph reminds me,
    Back garden romance with plastic roses
Ballet shoes and ringlets.
    A soldier stood next to me
Sword in scabbard
    Hand in mine
As we walked between the swings and
    Cathedral towers
A cracker ring
    Placed on my finger
A bond never to be forgotten
    On a summer's day
With childish dreams
    For a wedding in net curtains

A lesson in another school illustrates how the work can be organised, and the material planned, so as to make active demands on pupils. A group of fourth year pupils preparing for a CSE examination were given ten lines from Blake's *Auguries of Innocence*[8].

The babe that weeps the rod beneath
    writes revenge in realms of death.
The beggar's rags, fluttering in air,
    Does to rags the heavens tear.
The soldier, armed with sword and gun,
    Palsied strikes the summer's sun.

The strongest poison ever known
    Came from Caesar's laurel crown.
Nought can deform the human race
    Like to the armour's iron brace...

and W H Auden's *Epitaph on a Tyrant*[8]

> *Perfection, of a kind, was what he was after,*
>   *And the poetry he invented was easy to understand;*
> *He knew human folly like the back of his hand,*
>   *And was greatly interested in armies and fleets;*
> *When he laughed, respectable senators burst with laughter,*
>   *And when he cried the little children died in the streets.*

After an initial reading by the teacher, the pupils were divided into groups of four and asked to prepare two 'opinion' questions and two 'factual' questions about the Blake couplets and to decide what was Auden's opinion of the tyrant in the epitaph, using supporting evidence from the poem. Among the factual questions produced by the groups were; 'Who is wielding the rod in the first line?' 'What does "palsied" mean?' 'What is the poison referred to?' 'What is a laurel crown?' 'Who was Caesar?' The answers emerged readily from the class's combined efforts, except for 'palsied' which had to be looked up in a dictionary. The 'poison' question was answered obliquely by a boy's references to Napoleon in Orwell's *Animal Farm* which the class had read in the third year. The class were able to establish for themselves a layer of meaning and a working vocabulary from these questions. The opinion questions were both direct and indirect: 'Does the poet think that the babe and the beggar are badly treated?' 'Why are people cruel to children?' 'Should you give money to people poorer than you who need it?' There was sensible discussion of these questions, with a variety of views expressed and an acceptance that recognition of a poet's viewpoint entailed no obligation on the reader to think or feel the same way. The discussion which followed the teacher's question on the Auden poem showed the pupils' ability to read below the surface and to see through the depiction of the apparent reasonableness and ordinariness of power. There was a unanimous view that Auden was glad the tyrant was dead and most pupils adduced the last line as evidence of this. The teacher then explained that the two poets were separated by 150 years or there-abouts. If they should meet, he asked, would they have anything in common? In pairs the class were then asked to list the points of contact between the poems. Among the points raised by a number of groups were a dislike of cruelty, and the suffering of innocent people, often children, in political events, and the fear of individuals with too much power

11

which the teacher explained further by introducing the word 'absolute'. Prompted by the teacher, who read the poem aloud again, the pupils began to see how the use of rhyme made the views of the poets clearer still. Most children in the class agreed it did and were led to a consideration of the relationships between form and content. Thus their linguistic awareness was enlarged and their ability to take part in the great discourse we call reading was sharpened and extended.

In another school the pupils' attention was drawn specifically to the overtones and associations of different words by a consideration of two translations of a poem by the Russian writer Andrei Voznesensky.

FIRST ICE [9]

A girl freezes in a telephone booth.
In her draughty overcoat she hides
a face all smeared
In tears and lipstick.

She breathes on her thin palms.
Her fingers are icy. She wears earrings.

She'll have to go home alone, alone,
Along the icy street.

First ice. It is the first time.
The first ice of telephone phrases.

Frozen tears glitter on her cheeks –
The first ice of human hurt.

A girl is freezing in a telephone booth,
huddled in her flimsy coat,
her face stained by tears
and smeared with lipstick.

She breathes on her thin little fingers.
Fingers like ice. Glass beads in her ears.

She has to beat her way back alone
down the icy street.

First frost. A beginning of losses.
The first frost of telephone phrases.

It is the start of winter glittering on her cheek,
the first frost of having been hurt.

The pupils were asked to underline all the words which were different in the two versions, moving line by line through the poems; and then, in pairs, to discuss the different words used and to reach some conclusions, or at least exchange views, about their effectiveness. The sensitivity to subtleties and shades of meaning was thrown into sharp relief by the juxtaposition of words from each poem – 'draughty'/'flimsy', 'she hides'/'huddled' for example and the opportunity was thus given for involved and active reading. The pupils had also looked at drafts of Keats' Odes and some of Blake's Notebook poems and had been given the opportunity to see how poets improved and extended their meaning as part of a drafting process; and that for instance the replacement of 'dirty streets' by 'chartered streets' in Blake's *London* gave the poem a depth of reference and meaning which the first version lacked.

3

Talking about poetry
– 'minds traverse one another'

IT IS a fact, almost universally acknowledged, that exploratory talk by pupils has an important function in the process of learning. Keats in a letter to Reynolds made the point, with a sense more of its mystery than of its group dynamics, that 'Minds leave each other in contrary direction, traverse each other at numberless points and at last greet each other at the journey's end.' This process of accepting, absorbing and learning from each other can be a keynote of much successful poetry teaching. In the examples quoted above the pupils were, at carefully chosen moments and with specially prepared material, given opportunities to develop their own ideas, not simply to receive instruction from the teacher. In small group discussion the pupil can share insights, test hypotheses, be free to be mistaken and to learn from the rest of the group. James Britton's comment on talk in the classroom, though made in a general context, holds good for all work in English and in particular poetry: 'Anyone who succeeded in outlawing talk in the classroom would have outlawed life for the adolescent: the web of human relations must be spun in school as well as out'. The extract which follows is from a tape transcript of five third year pupils in an Oxfordshire school discussing *The Warm and the Cold* by Ted Hughes.

Freezing dusk is closing
Like a slow trap of steel
On trees and roads and hills and all
That can no longer feel.
    But the carp is in its depth
    Like a planet in its heaven.
    And the badger in its bedding
    Like a loaf in the oven.
    And the butterfly in its mummy
    Like a viol in its case.
    And the owl in its feathers
    Like a doll in its lace.

Freezing dusk has tightened
Like a nut screwed tight
On the starry aeroplane
Of the soaring night.
    But the trout is in its hole
    Like a chuckle in a sleeper.
    The hare strays down the highway
    Like a root going deeper.
    The snail is dry in the outhouse
    Like a seed in a sunflower.
    The owl is pale on the gatepost
    Like a clock on its tower.

Moonlight freezes the shaggy world
Like a mammoth of ice –
The past and the future
Are the jaws of a steel vice.
    But the cod is in the tide-rip
    Like a key in a purse.
    The deer are on the bare-blown hill
    Like smiles on a nurse.
    The flies are behind the plaster
    Like the lost score of a jig.
    Sparrows are in the ivy-clump
    Like money in a pig.

Such a frost
The flimsy moon
Has lost her wits.

A star falls.

The sweating farmers
Turn in their sleep
Like oxen on spits.

Graham[12]	So the lost score, the score is what it's written on – it's the music.
Zoe	So they lost it, nobody knows what it is.
Tom	Eh?
Nick	Everything's coming to an end at the end of the day.
Tom	Oh yes sort of –
Nick	Everything's sort of slowing down 'til it stops.
Tom	Yeah!
Graham	The day, the day's sort of a dance
Tom	and dusk's the last bit of it.
Graham	'The deer on the ...' What about 'the deer on the bare-blown hill/like smiles on a nurse'?
Zoe	I don't get that.

16

Graham	No, it doesn't seem like all this. The others kind of relate – the cod, and the key in the purse, kind of relate more than 'the deer on ...'
Tom	Yeah, What is ... I mean it's got fish in all three here – 'the carp's in its depth/like a planet in its heaven' then 'the trout's in its hole/like a chuckle in a sleeper' ... erm, and 'the cod's in the tide rip/like a key in a purse'. It must all relate somehow.
Graham	The first verse is always fish.
Tom	You know, the first bit of it.
Graham	Yes, the first line, up here you've got the first four lines then you've got fish.
Zoe	The last one's always – a bird.
Tom	Yeah, and then you've got ...
Zoe	Badger and all the mammals.
Tom	Yeah and you've got a lot about steel in there as well – 'the slow trap of steel' ... erm You got badger 'jaws of a steel vice'
Graham	Badger
Zoe	Hare
Lucy	and deer
Tom	We're paying a lot of attention to what he's said.
Nick	and music as well. (Inaudible) ... things 'cos you've got a clock in its tower –
Graham	It's all natural
Nick	– and sparrows in the ivy clump
Tom	Yeah, what about.
Nick	– then it's got 'doll in its lace'
Zoe	It's sort of all relating where they live
Tom	Yeah and music as well 'like a viol in its case' ... erm –
Graham	It all matches as if –
Tom	– and ... erm – 'lost score of a jig'
Graham	Apart from the flies behind the plaster, that sounds quite different.

17

Tom	Yeah, I can't understand that.
Zoe	and the smiles on the nurse, I don't understand
Graham	'The flies are behind the plaster' is different, the rest of them are –
Tom	Yeah, I don't understand things like 'The deer on the bare blown hill/like smiles on a nurse.' I mean what are they?

The extract shows pupils exploring and establishing meaning for themselves, reading with intelligence and sensitivity, catching the rhythmic momentum and unfolding of the poem, alert to its images from within their reading. Such small group work is not a panacea and will not be successful if it is not a familiar part of work in English, carefully prepared and structured and leavened by judicious intervention by the teacher to give direction and support. But it can lead to deeper, more independent reading which is a necessary balance to the ransacking for content in the interests of what is paraphrasable which characterises much of the unenlightened preparation for public examinations. It is important that pupils are not tacitly encouraged to subordinate their own reading and experience of a poem to a form of words that it is believed will secure an examination pass. Discussion, whether in small groups or differently organised, shifts the emphasis from *teaching poetry* to *learning how to read and experience poetry*; it shows that many pupils have an original contribution to make because of what each uniquely brings to the reading, and it fosters a process that is central to English teaching in the secondary years.

Whatever directions are taken it is clear, as was stated above, that the presentation of poetry in the secondary school needs to be carefully planned and provided for. The planning needs to include a detailed consideration of a wide variety of ways of presenting poetry in the classroom. Providing for it should set out to create the context in which the presentation and experience of poetry can flourish. In most schools not enough of this is done to make poetry available. Library stocks are often meagre; sixth form libraries may contain the poets set for examination but often lack much primary and basic textual material, having duplicate copies of low level critical 'crib' material rather than a good collection of the work of poets writing at the present time and a full range of major poets from Chaucer onwards. It is rare to see poetry books on display in school libraries or for pupils' own writing to be linked to displays of collections of poetry.

In specialist English rooms much more could be done to give pupils the opportunity to assemble and display their own choice of poems, to provide individual copies of poems which might interest, to draw pupils' attention to poets who live or have lived in the neighbourhood or who may have used the locality in their work. Some schools enterprisingly have held poetry festivals and have used the visit of a poet to the school to read his work to imprint the claims of poetry firmly on the school through a series of related activities:- staff and pupils reading their favourite poems in the lunch hour, well-known poems duplicated and displayed in social areas of the school, promoting the sale of poetry books through the school bookshop, pupils writing, editing and producing their own poetry magazine. These activities are not, simply, the background to the teaching of poetry; rather they are the foreground, the mould in which the experience of poetry is cast.

4

Developing the
auditory imagination

POETRY IS rooted in an oral tradition and poetry in schools can endeavour to restore something of its traditional public and rhetorical voice through performance. Donne's *Songs and Sonnets* and Blake's *Songs of Innocence and Experience* remind us of the connections between poetry and song and activities engendered in the classroom should bring the sound of poetry to pupils' ears. In the first instance teachers need to read poetry aloud well, and to exploit their capacities for doing so, but the pupils' experience should extend to preparations for reading aloud and performance. For a group of pupils to consider how they are going to read a poem aloud means they become closely involved with meaning and the expression of meaning: they experience the power of alliteration, hear assonance, rhyme and rhythm at first hand and absorb in the most obvious and common-sense way what are often taught as remote technical features. If pupils are asked to prepare programmes of poetry for particular audiences the selection of suitable material becomes a critical process which asks questions about suitability and difficulty and can only be answered by students on the basis of their informed reading and perception of occasion and audience. What poems might a fifth year group choose for a tape-recorded poetry programme for first year pupils? If a group of pupils prepares material for a live reading for a local old people's home, or for a programme about Christmas for a hospital radio station, what considerations might inform their selection and balance of material?

The dimension of performing poetry gives to pupils an opportunity to experience the operation of those technical and formal devices which have for so long been the subject of irrelevant classification in the classroom. These terms (rhyme, rhythm, alliteration, assonance, metaphor, simile, imagery and many more obscured in the language of Greek prosody) cannot be ignored in the exploration and establishment of meaning, but they must stem naturally from the organic whole of the poem and not be seen as ingredients placed in solemn proportions in the poetic mixing bowl and then stirred.

Poetic rhythm has its roots in the patterns of ordinary speech, more highly and consciously organised, but not applied from outside. The 'auditory imagination' as T S Eliot called it, is a feeling for rhythm and syllable 'below the level of conscious thought'. To develop a response to this it is essential for pupils to be given the opportunities to hear the words as a pattern of articulate sounds, to read with the ear as well as the eye and to recognise that rhythmic effects are only part of a number of other subtle and elusive aspects of poetic language. Pupils can apprehend that rhythm sets up a pattern of expectation in the regularity of a pattern of stresses, as part of their experiences of reading. They will sense, too, that rhythm in poetry reinforces meaning and that stress patterns derive from the normal pronunciation of words, with the normal emphasis of everyday speech. Pupils best exercise the auditory imagination by regular reading and listening to whole poems read aloud. In a sixth form college, each student in turn was expected to spend at least one hour on a prepared reading of a poem of his or her choice, every week. Reading the poem aloud was the introductory part of the lesson which the student conducted, giving thoughts, perceptions and responses to the poem. For one boy, the work on the preparation for reading aloud had given him a key to the poem he had chosen – *View of a Pig* by Ted Hughes: 'As I read this poem aloud the words had the sound of flesh on flesh to me. It seemed to me that Hughes was, in essence, slapping and kicking this inert mound with his words. I couldn't hear this as I read it silently in my head'.

The effects of rhyme and rhythm are closely connected with sound and verbal patterns; metaphor by contrast is concerned with the meanings of words and is at the centre of poetic expression. Metaphor has been called 'the swift illumination of an equivalence', a comparison which involves the mind of the reader in a positive act of interpretation between the attributes of the things compared. Living metaphor also shocks and surprises the reader by its audacity, stopping us in our tracks and causing us to delve and explore. Lists of worn similes and metaphors learned by heart lose all this force. Thus pupils can, by their experience of reading, be brought to the point where they are able to enter into the nature of the implied comparison. One approach would be to alert children to the fact that everyday language is full of metaphors – 'You rat', 'Don't be wet', 'You're throwing away your chances', 'Let's float the idea', 'I'm heart-broken', 'There's something in the wind', 'I can't make head or tail of it' – and examples can be collected and displayed. In this way pupils will realise that metaphor is deeply embedded in language: the act of reading metaphor makes them aware of the comparison between familiar things, and this presents a new dimension and precision to feeling and experience. For poetry does not simply make statements. It takes the reader into the re-creation of experience; and metaphor, in a subtle and flexible way, draws the reader into understanding by causing this active and positive response. In this way, pupils can become aware of the special emotional and imaginative control a poet achieves when the familiar and everyday metaphors of ordinary speech no longer suffice, when the pressure of experience creates its own originality:

> *Life's but a walking shadow; a poor player,*
> *That struts and frets his hour upon the stage,*
> *And then is heard no more: it is a tale*
> *Told by an idiot, full of sound and fury,*
> *Signifying nothing.*

Macbeth Act V, Scene V

It was argued in the opening paragraphs that poetry is important because it has qualities of utterance pupils need to experience if they are to become more aware of the possibilities of language. Insight into poetry grows with insight into language and the processes are mutually supporting. Approaches to poetry in the classroom can make children aware of the wide range of emotional possibilities each word possesses according to its context, its speaker, its association or its history. Indeed just as it can be pointed out that metaphor – an apparently remote term – is deeply rooted in ordinary speech, so pupils, through looking at the examples around them in advertising and the press, can readily perceive how the emotional reverberations of language and its potency as a purveyor of ideas and images are exploited for particular effect. They will recognise similarly that poets for rather different reasons work with conscious thought and rigour in forming their words into a powerful creative order, which often depends strongly on association and context. It has been argued that reading poetry is a discovery or creation of its meaning and that reading poetry aloud heightens the sense of its unity and organic quality whereby the whole is more than the sum of constituent parts. So if insight into the possibilities of language is a product of the experiencing of it, it is important through the sustained reading and discussion of poetry to give pupils the chance to become more linguistically alert, competent and adventurous, bringing their own experiences, thought and rigour to bear on, and combine with, the poets they read. It is this influence which Seamus Heaney described in his image of 'words entering the echo chamber of your head'.

5

Finding a voice

IN A sense all writing connected with the experience of poetry is creative, when it is the pupils' own, whether it is evaluative and analytic or expressive and poetic. Wherever pupils are themselves involved in placing this word next to that, there can be expressions of freshness of thought and feeling. It is important that pupils' writing is not confined to an unduly narrow framework and that a range of possibilities is seen to be available and to be equally valued for the language and insights which they generate. Children need to experience the placing of words together so that they can become 'makers' for themselves. A girl in a Nottinghamshire school was asked where her words came from in her own complex and luxuriant writing. She replied 'I just pick them up – out of the books I read, really – and I use them every now and then. Everything I read has a good word in it and I fix that word in my mind so that I won't forget it'. It is a function of poetry in school to feed pupils' store of words so that when they write themselves they become absorbed in the 'fascination of what's difficult', in the assembly of what Ted Hughes calls the living parts of language.

The point is illustrated by the writing of a fifteen year old pupil from a Northamptonshire comprehensive school. The class had been reading poetry extensively for half a term and were encouraged, in their responses, to work in a variety of ways, including experiments in the form, but not necessarily using the substance, of a poem they had read which had caught their interest. One pupil took Ted Hughes' *Hawk Roosting* and made of it a striking vision:

I stand above the rest, watching intensely.
Inaction no falsifying dream
Between my pressed suit and polished shoes:
Or in a sleep rehearse stern looks and nos.

The convenience of house buyers!
The light room and large windows
Are of advantage to me;
And the people look up to me, so nervous

My fists are clenched around leather arms.
It took a Nation of investors
To produce my desk, my each clerk:
Now I hold the Nation in my fist

Or drive and admire it keenly –
I stop where I please, because it is all mine.
There is no laughter on my lips:
My matters are the selling of money –

The allotment of debt
For the one path of my success is direct
Through the pockets of the classes.
No arguments assert my right:

Power is behind me.
Only money has changed since I began.
My pen has permitted that change.
I am going to keep things like this.

Such control over form and idea could not have come about without a prolonged immersion in the reading of the original poetry, whose 'echoes' have given a new dimension to the writing. In a similar way, a group of girls in a secondary school in Southall had been exploring, through their reading of Seamus Heaney's poetry, ideas of language, background and tradition, finding in Heaney's Irish context a parallel with their own awareness of their roots in the Punjab. After a careful reading and discussion, in a small group, of *Digging* and *Follower*, Amita wrote of her own experience of generations.

WASHING [14]

Round and round, round and round
Circles of white soap suds,
Cleansing the plate thoroughly,
Her hands tender and soft wiping the dishes
As though massaging an oily body.

Such perfection was there in her every move,
Not a mistake, but working like a programmed robot,
That constant circular movement seemed to
Recall memories.

Yes, I recognised the movements,
It was so familiar,
It was her mother I remember who washed in
Such perfection just like her.

It was almost as if she had adopted her mother's arms,
Her tall, slim body swayed slightly as she
Continued to cleanse the plates,
The movement still going – round and round.

She opened the tap as the steaming hot water,
Steam, rose filling the air with a cosy feeling,
Tenderly she rinsed away the foamy soap suds,
They collected at the bottom of the sink gurgling down,
Another plate,
Yet again – round and round – round and round,
That same generational adopted move.

The following poem was written by a 12 year old after a lengthy class discussion about Blake's poem *A Poison Tree* and demonstrates a 'process of creation in response to the poet's words', a moment of identification with its own passionate weight, reflecting a complex and intellectual reading.

HATRED

You silently mouth words you will never say
And tears run down your cheek, hot like your hatred.
And yet they hurt twice as much as tears of sorrow,
Your tears of fury.
You silently clench your hands, for a blow you will never strike,
And plunge into an unreal heart.
And when the world laughs unreal laughs
You pray that you'll be lifted out to die.

There is a certain dignified melancholy in the structure of Simon's poem which was part of a project on The Vikings and which had used Gregory Harrison's *Night Attack* as a starting point for a range of spoken and written work.

The King's retainers carry the body
   To the sea where his long ship is waiting.
On the pyre his body is laid,
   All his belongings by him,
Out into the open sea

Slowly the pyre sets alight
   And out to sea it drifts
As the night draws in, the ship
   Fades far away under the sea.

Writing generated by close study of an author for A-level work may take forms quite different from the multitude of featureless and pre-packaged answers to A-level questions, produced in what are believed to be appropriate responses to examination needs. *Mordred's Lament*, written by an A-level pupil after reading Malory, is evidence of the intertwining of critical and creative responses into a blended vision, illuminating the original text and taking the writer into new areas of language where he can demonstrate its vitality at first hand.

MORDRED'S LAMENT

Age 17 ... after reading Malory

I am the ill made knight
   I spider, stooping heavy
of jaw, weak of eye, coughing
      through the dark, soggy-twigged woods
of our circumstance.
            The hounds
      cringe from my hand: my shadow
in torchlight scares the gossamer ladies;
      what friends I have had are spurred
away, by my blank silences
      or by my slobbering furies
that erupt like grey, bloody fat
      from a cloven head.
            When the king calls us
around the blazoned wheel of the table,
      Lancelot a spear of bronze
by his side, to chart new schemes
      in defeat of the wolves from the grey sea
I sit, dully. The gnat in my skull
      whispers as always
            'What good is all this?'
and the moist dazzle in the eyes
      of my noble comrades, never reaches
mine. My sword is lost, hidden
      on the worn, dripping stone.

O gods
gods of trees and springs
gods of mistletoe and golden sickle
gods of tapestried altars
help my unbelief, for I have lost sight
of the shining Grail.

The teacher has a vital role to play in helping pupils in all the stages of their writing, in their experiments, tentative formulations, processes of clarifying meaning and expression. There is now general agreement that the unthinking assumptions of 'When in doubt, write a poem' are no longer good enough, although it is still common to find choices for pupils' writing ending with 'Or you may write a poem if you wish' as though it required no special preparation or effort. The close connections between reading and writing poetry demonstrate the proper seriousness of the matter, as ideas and feelings are wrought into expressive form. Though tactful, sensitive and positive, the teacher must not receive pupils' work with easy and sentimental praise. Pupils as writers need the benefit of clear and frank appraisal, an expectation that they will re-work ideas in sections of their writing, and plenty of time and encouragement to do so. It follows that teachers need to be sure of their judgements, to be widely read in poetry themselves, and perhaps to be engaged in the business of writing themselves alongside their pupils from time to time. Not least, they must be critically discerning enough to recognise a voice the pupil owns and to be able to distinguish it from one that has been rented for the occasion, and to be alert to those moments in a child's writing when there is an important shift in capability and consciousness.

Teachers have a responsibility to make sure their own models of what is to be valued are not stranded in stale and sterile forms. It is of course true that the outcome of poetry teaching need not be writing at all, and that many poems can be read just for themselves, as an experience of the moment, whose echoes for some will last into the future. But the evidence is that a rich and varied experience of poetry will engender in most pupils the desire to write; to seek to close the gap between their experiences and the words that are available to give them shape. The four poems which follow, produced by pupils in schools, have that quality of complexity that reveals, in Ted Hughes' phrase, 'the vital signature of a human being'.

29

Jennifer Mitchell

Deflating like a Michelin man,
my mother's home-truths acting
as a penknife – ripping ego.
Reflecting, the mirror tells no lies –
the body like a topless pear,
hips ready for virgin childbirth,
an hourglass with no link
between the hours.
Cheeks with the fat
of a thousand babies, non-existent
cheekbones, the suggestion
of a moustache
(the curse of every beauty queen).
Perched on a small plum,
the glasses thick enough
to enlarge the pupils, bulge the eyes.

The home-truths hitting home

THE SINGER (STANDING STONE) [16]

Sarah Childs (17)

The world passes you by,
Sit, as you sing, smiling,
A life in each red gold tangled hair,
The cobbles hard beneath you.

Sit, as you sing, smiling,
Your guitar apricot
In the scudding sun,
In your blue green eyes holding
All the tears ever wrung.

Sit, as you sing, smiling,
And the people pass you by,
Your voice holds in a million years,
Your heart, a million skies.

Sit, as you sing, smiling,
Forever I see you there.
The church may crumble,
But on the hill,
The man with the songs fills the air.

FROG 16

Lisa Robinson (13)

It sits, a moist ball of flesh in my hand
Vulnerable, pressed belly close to my pink palm,
The ball of putty croaks
Blowing out with care, his throat balloon taut.
He lets it go shrivelling back into limp folds
Like worn material.
He hangs his skin cravat under his chin and smiles.
Suddenly his head jerks up
Sending black warts colliding down his back.
His eyes swivel
Full of wet black wonder
Exaggerated by the thin circlet of gold he wears
    around them
Regally he stands
In wait for the worm, long pale pink innocence.
Then tongue whips the air and satisfaction slips down
His throat.
He presses his eyes down and shuffles his
    membraneous feet
He smiles and rests his head flaccidly on my thumb.

David Woodhouse (14)

Nocker Norton,
Balding albino tiger,
The Boulevard mud
Does not lust for your body
As expected.

The inevitable massive tackle
Does not spread its muddy, muscled grasp
Around another passive Titan
As expected.

But instead flashes like
A laser beam from
Your tinkling fingertips.
The crowd
Loves you
As expected.

In the work of these young writers the reader feels the pressure of human experience and responds to the presence of such creative energy. But work of such quality and personal and linguistic integrity does not simply happen. In the experience that lies behind writing like this there lie those encounters with books and poems which, in Kafka's words, act 'as an ice-axe to break the sea frozen inside us'. By feeling both closeness and continuity with writers who connect with us across gaps of historical time, children find their own originality in the dignity, resources and uses of language. In this way they can themselves begin to make sense of the world in which we live. If literature is the expression of a human dimension and connection then the experience of it should not be a matter of chance but of entitlement.

Notes and References

1   The extract is reprinted by permission of Faber and Faber and is taken from Seamus Heaney's book *Preoccupation: selected prose 1968–78*. Faber and Faber, 1980.

2   HMI are indebted to Mr J. Ousby, General Adviser, Nottinghamshire, for this quotation.

3   *See* Baldick, C. *The social mission of English criticism*. Oxford University Press, 1983 for an illuminating and detailed discussion of the development of English as a classroom subject.

4   Hughes, Ted. *Poetry in the making : an anthology of poems and programmes from 'Listening and Writing'*. Faber and Faber, 1969.

5   The Bullock Report. *A language for life*. HMSO, 1975.

6   Assessment of Performance Unit (APU). *Language performance in schools : secondary survey report No. 1*. HMSO, 1982.
    Details of APU's work and publications are available from APU, Room 4/77a, Elizabeth House, York Road, London SE1 7PH.

7   Wright, Kit. *The bear looked over the mountain*. Salamander Imprint, 1977. The poem is reproduced by permission of the author.

8 The passages are both *in* Heaney, Seamus and Hughes, Ted. *The rattlebag.* Faber and Faber, 1983. *Epitaph on a Tyrant* is reprinted by permission of Faber and Faber from W.H. Auden's book *Collected poems.* Faber and Faber, 1976.

9 Translated by George Reavey and included *in* Barnstone, Willis (Ed.) *Modern European poetry.* Bantam, 1966. Copyright © 1966, 1978 by Bantam Books Inc. Reprinted by permission of the publishers.

10 Translated by Stanley Kunitz and included *in* Blake, Patricia and Hayward, Max (Eds.) *Antiworlds and the fifth ace: poems by Andrei Voznesensky.* A bilingual edition with a foreword by W.H. Auden. Copyright © 1966, 1967 by Basic Books Inc. Publishers Copyright © 1963 by Encounter Ltd. The poem is reprinted by permission of the publishers.

11 *The Warm and the Cold* is reprinted by permission of Faber and Faber and is included in Ted Hughes' book *Season songs.* Faber and Faber, 1976.

12 HMI are grateful to Dr P. Benton for permission to use this extract from his research material. The findings of his research project were published under the title *Pupil, teacher, poem* by Hodder and Stoughton, 1986.

13 HMI are grateful to Mrs P. Barnard, curriculum advisory teacher in Northamptonshire, for permission to use this poem.

14 HMI are grateful to Mr M. Harrison for permission to include this poem.

15 Included in *City lines: poems by London school students.* ILEA English Centre, 1982. The poem is reproduced by permission of the author.

16 These poems are to be found in *Cadbury's second book of children's poetry.* Beaver, 1984. They are reproduced by permission of Cadbury Ltd.

Printed for Her Majesty's Stationery Office by Hobbs the Printers of Southampton
(158/87) Dd239860 C100 3/87 G3379